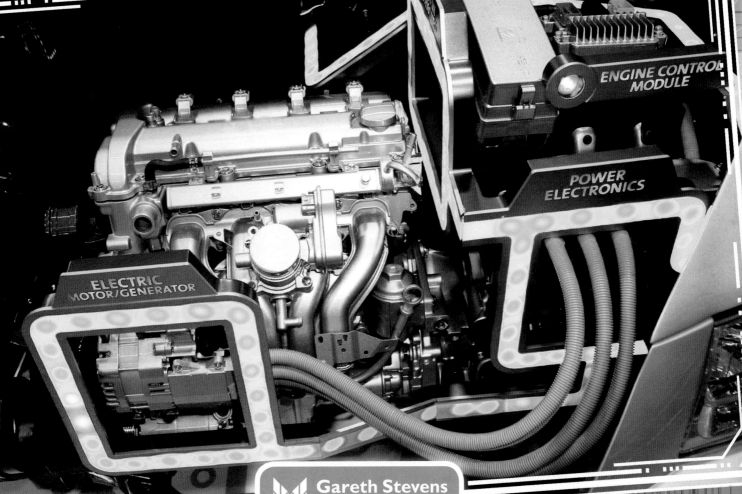

MOTORS AND GENERATORS

ENGINE CONTROL MODULE

POWER ELECTRONICS

ELECTRIC MOTOR/GENERATOR

Gareth Stevens Publishing

By Grace Vail

Please visit our website, www.garethstevens.com. For a free color catalog of all our high-quality books, call toll free 1-800-542-2595 or fax 1-877-542-2596.

Library of Congress Cataloging-in-Publication Data

Vail, Grace.
  Motors and generators / Grace Vail.
      p. cm. — (Electrified!)
  Includes index.
  ISBN 978-1-4339-8405-1 (pbk.)
  ISBN 978-1-4339-8406-8 (6-pack)
  ISBN 978-1-4339-8404-4 (library binding)
  1. Electric motors—Juvenile literature. 2. Electric generators—Juvenile literature. I. Title.
  TK9911.V325 2013
  621.46—dc23

                              2012023549

First Edition

Published in 2013 by
Gareth Stevens Publishing
111 East 14th Street, Suite 349
New York, NY 10003

Copyright © 2013 Gareth Stevens Publishing

Designer: Katelyn E. Reynolds
Editor: Therese Shea

Photo credits: Cover, p. 1 © iStockphoto.com/GreenPimp; cover, pp. 1 (logo), 4, 15, 19 (inset) 20 iStockphoto/Thinkstock.com; cover, pp. 1, 3–24 (background) Lukas Radavicius/Shutterstock.com; cover, pp. 1, 3–24 (image frame) VikaSuh/Shutterstock.com; p. 5 Andrew Olney/Photodisc/Thinkstock.com; p. 7 rimira/Shutterstock.com; p. 9 Hemera/Thinkstock.com; pp. 11, 17 Dorling Kindersley RF/Thinkstock.com; p. 13 Adam Crowley/Photodisc/Thinkstock.com; p. 19 (main) Jay Directo/AFP/Getty Images; p. 21 Top Photo Group/Thinkstock.com.

Printed in the United States of America

CPSIA compliance information: Batch #CW13GS: For further information contact Gareth Stevens, New York, New York at 1-800-542-2595.

CONTENTS

Words in the glossary appear in **bold** type the first time they are used in the text.

MAKING IT WORK

What do a washing machine, hair dryer, blender, and refrigerator all have in common? They have motors! Almost any electric tool with moving parts has a motor. All these machines probably use electricity produced by a generator, too.

Knowing more about motors and generators can teach you a lot about electricity. For example, did you know that magnets are a key part of making electricity? It's true! Motors and generators couldn't work without the force of magnetism.

washing machine motor

Many household machines get power, or energy, from another source. Motors and generators provide different kinds of energy.

MAGNETS MAKE IT MOVE

If you've ever played with magnets, you know they can make metals move. A magnet is a metal, too. It has two poles—a north pole and a south pole. Like poles of magnets **repel** each other, and opposite poles **attract** each other. The north pole of a magnet attracts the south pole of another magnet, but it repels another north pole. The area around the magnet affected by this magnetic force is called the magnetic field.

Some objects become magnets when electricity runs through them. These are called electromagnets.

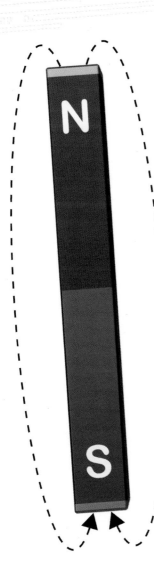

ELECTROMAGNETS

Most electromagnets are made of at least two **conductors**, such as a copper wire wrapped around an iron rod. When an electric **current** flows through the wire, the wire becomes an electromagnet. It has the properties of a regular magnet, including a magnetic field and two poles.

A simple motor uses an electromagnet and a regular magnet. The electromagnet moves. The regular magnet is fixed in place. It's called the field magnet. The motor changes, or converts, electrical energy into mechanical energy using these magnets.

POWER FACT!

In large motors, the field magnet may be an electromagnet as well. Some motors even have several field magnets.

The more **coils** wrapped around the metal rod, the stronger the magnetic field of an electromagnet is.

9

KEEP IT MOVING

The movement of the electromagnet is what makes the motor work. Current running through an electromagnet causes it to **rotate** until its north pole is opposite the field magnet's south pole. Of course, this one movement isn't enough to make the motor work. The movement must continue.

So to keep the electromagnet moving, the current keeps switching direction. This makes the electromagnet's poles switch. The electromagnet must keep turning to match its poles to the opposite poles of the field magnet.

POWER FACT!

The motor is connected to the machine it's running by a **driveshaft**.

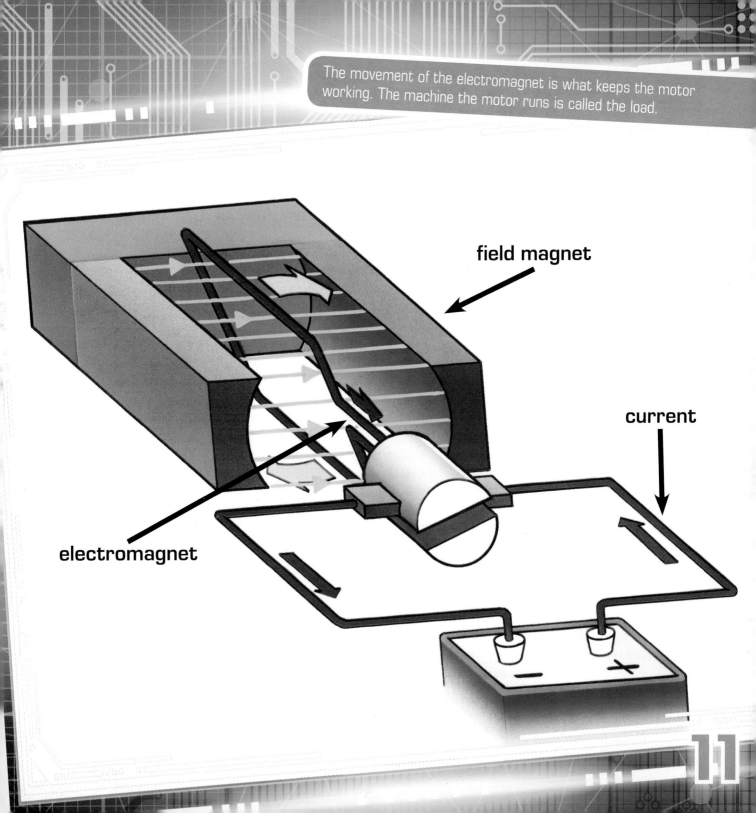

The movement of the electromagnet is what keeps the motor working. The machine the motor runs is called the load.

field magnet

current

electromagnet

AC AND DC

How does the current switch directions in a motor? This depends on whether the electricity running the motor is AC or DC. AC means "alternating current." This flow of electricity usually **reverses** about 60 times per second. So the current switches directions by itself and keeps the motor's electromagnet moving.

DC means "direct current." This electricity flows in one direction. When the electromagnet in a DC motor moves to a certain point, a special **device** reverses the current's direction.

POWER FACT!

Most motors are built to operate on either AC or DC electricity. However, a universal motor can use either AC or DC.

Your home probably has AC electricity running from its outlets. Batteries are an example of DC electricity.

13

POWER UP!

Most of the electricity you use each day comes from generators. Huge power plant generators can supply power for entire cities. Small generators may have enough to power a small home.

A generator changes mechanical energy into electrical energy. A device such as a **turbine** (like in a windmill) or an engine (like in a car) makes the mechanical energy. Different sources of energy drive this device. Heat, steam, and water provide the needed power for some generators.

Wind power turns the blades of this turbine.
The generator inside produces electricity.

15

PRODUCING CURRENT

The mechanical energy in the generator produces electricity. How does this happen? Just as in motors, generators use the properties of magnetism.

In a simple generator, the turbine, engine, or other device rotates a coil of wire, usually copper, within a field magnet's magnetic field. The movement produces, or generates, an electric current through the wire. There are AC and DC generators of electricity.

POWER FACT!

Trains and ships often use DC generators.

ELECTRICITY ON THE GO

What happens to the electricity after a power plant generator makes it? The current travels through a system of power lines. Devices called transformers raise and lower the **voltage** at certain points. High voltage helps current travel far. Lower voltage is safer for your home.

When the current reaches your home, it travels through the wires inside the walls. You use the electricity when you flip a **switch**, or plug in or turn on a device.

POWER FACT!

Coal, natural gas, and oil are **fossil fuels** burned to create heat or steam, which powers most power plant generators.

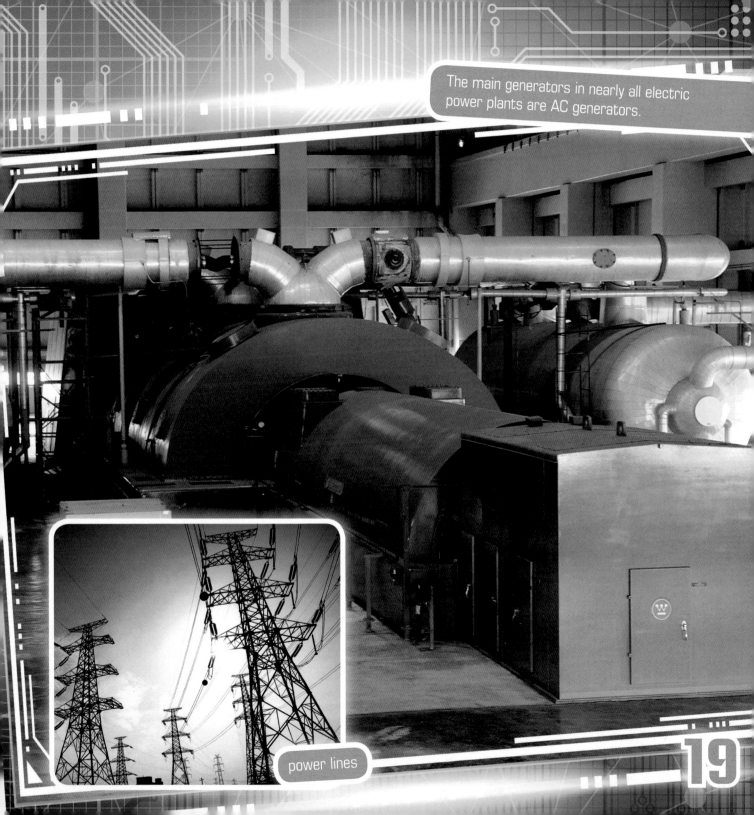

The main generators in nearly all electric power plants are AC generators.

power lines

19

WORKING TOGETHER

Most motors in your home wouldn't work without the electricity from power plant generators. Remember, motors need electrical energy to make mechanical energy. It's easy to see some motors at work. For example, a motor spins the blades of a ceiling fan.

Sometimes you can hear motors at work. A refrigerator motor hums. It helps keeps the temperature inside low so food doesn't spoil. Cars, buses, and trains use both motors and generators and can be very noisy. Quiet, loud, seen, or unseen—motors and generators make our lives easier!

GLOSSARY

attract: to draw nearer

coil: a series of loops

conductor: matter through which electricity flows easily

current: a flow of electricity resulting from the movement of particles such as electrons

device: a tool or machine made to perform a task

driveshaft: a turning rod that provides motion or power for a machine

fossil fuel: matter formed over millions of years from plant and animal remains that is burned for power

repel: to push away

reverse: to move in the opposite direction

rotate: to turn around a fixed point

switch: a device that opens, closes, or changes the connections in an electrical circuit

turbine: a motor operated by the movement of water, steam, or air

voltage: a measurement of electrical energy

FOR MORE INFORMATION

Books

Hartman, Eve, and Wendy Meshbesher. *Magnetism and Electromagnets.* Chicago, IL: Raintree, 2009.

Parker, Steve. *Energy and Power.* Broomall, PA: Mason Crest, 2011.

Websites

Generators, Batteries, and Solar Cells

idahoptv.org/dialogue4kids/season6/electricity/generator.cfm

Read about generators and other sources of energy.

How Electric Motors Work

www.howstuffworks.com/motor.htm

Find out more about motors and their different parts.

Moving Electrons and Charges

www.physics4kids.com/files/elec_intro.html

Want to know exactly what electricity is? Check out this site.

INDEX